MW01051225

REFERRALS MADE EASY

It's just <u>NOT</u> that hard!

Robert E. Krumroy, CLU, ChFC

"I started highlighting from the first sentence in the preface. Krumroy is right ... it just isn't that hard, yet it is so critical. These ideas work!"

John T. Baier
CLU, ChFC, CFP®, MSFS, Managing Partner
New York Life Insurance Company

"If you're not getting the referral success you want, read this book! Its simple format, embraced by our agents, is producing significant referral results. It should be a mandatory read for all new agents!"

Donald Molineu Jr.
FICF, LLIF, South Carolina State Manager
Woodmen of the World

"The book lives up to its title. It's not only 'easy' but it is 'easily' transferable. This book will help the growth and retention of every agent and financial organization."

Ken Gallacher
LUTCF, CLF, FSS, Regional Director-Pacific Intermountain Region
American National Family of Companies

"Krumroy gets it right. This book proves how simple it is to unleash the tremendous referral value clients can easily provide. Referrals Made Easy is an exceptional book!"

T. Scott Newman
CLF, Branch Manager and recipient of GAMA's First in Class Award for 2008,
12 GAMA International Management Awards

Referrals Made Easy. It's just NOT that hard!

©2011 by Robert E. Krumroy

Publish date: February 2011

Given the current legal environment, we suggest that you consult your compliance or legal advisors before adapting the ideas presented in this book. We have not intentionally included any advice or materials that put you at risk, but we also realize how quickly and often laws and regulations change regarding the financial services industry.

This book is for general information purposes. Your company's compliance policies, procedures and initiatives will govern over any marketing strategies presented in this book that deviate from them.

Before any ideas are implemented, all correspondence and materials used with prospects or clients must be compliance-approved. The terms "advisor," "agent," "professional" and "representative" may appear in this book. Please check with your compliance department for appropriate terminology when using any of these terms in printed format.

This publication is designed to provide accurate and authoritative information in regard to the subject matter covered. It is sold with the understanding that neither the author nor the publisher is engaged in rendering legal, accounting or other professional service. If legal advice or other expert assistance is required, the services of a competent professional person should be sought. – From a Declaration of Principles jointly adopted by the American Bar Association and a committee of publishers.

I-B Publishing, Greensboro, NC

ISBN: 978-0-9678661-8-5

About the Author

Robert E. Krumroy

CEO, author of six books and founder of Identity Branding, Inc. and e-Relationship, has been teaching the principles of prospect attraction to financial sales professionals for more than 30 years. His impressive career placed him among the top 100 financial managers in the financial industry. Referred to as The Prospect-Attraction Coach, Robert is a nationally recognized speaker and teacher. The powerful strategy he teaches has dramatically improved sales, prospect  access, retention and recruiting for many of the leading financial service companies in the U.S. He lives in Greensboro, NC.

Table of Contents

Special Thanks

PREFACE   XI

The 10 Most Frequently Asked Questions About Referrals

Answers to the Most Frequently Asked Questions About Referrals

CHAPTER ONE   1

The Referral Mandate – Get Them!

CHAPTER TWO   5

Find Your Turning Point

CHAPTER THREE   11

The Dynamics of How to Ask for Referrals

CHAPTER FOUR   17

The Referral Script for Today's Client

CHAPTER FIVE   23

When Your Referral Request Is Denied

CHAPTER SIX   27

Introductions to Referrals are Critical – Agree on the Process!

CHAPTER SEVEN   31

Creating Clients to Become Consistent Referral Givers

PROLOGUE   43

ADVISOR TOOLBOX   49

Special Thanks

Special thanks to the people who provided the encouragement to address the issue of getting referrals.

The industry has allowed it to get way too complex.

The truth is … It's just NOT that hard.

Keep it simple.

PREFACE

The agent with superior talent rarely wins; the agent with superior positioning does. That's why not getting referrals will dwarf your success. If you are not willing to get referrals, look for a new career. This one will be dramatically handicapped in its ability to deliver what you want financially.

On a positive note, learning to get referrals is easy, and keeping them flowing is easy. Yes … *easy!* And it is the only way to become a super producer. Don't believe otherwise.

Learning to get referrals doesn't require spending a fortune on an expensive course. It doesn't require learning a myriad of replies to overcome objections. It doesn't require you to watch multiple videos for weeks on end. It doesn't require you to join a weekly peer group that promises to shame you into performing.

Referrals are your greatest leverage for superior production. There is no substitute!

What getting referrals does require is learning a simple strategy that can be mastered in 15 minutes. And it does require that, regardless of your moment of emotional anxiety, you stop wimping out.

If you're not willing to commit to asking and learning the simple referral-getting process that will produce results, don't read this book. It won't do any good. Your success or failure is a personal choice, and it begins with your level of commitment.

The 10 Most Frequently Asked Questions About Referrals

1. How important is a three-part referral script to my success?

2. Has the industry made referral asking more complicated than necessary?

3. How can I take the "scary" out of referral asking?

4. What do I do if my client says "no" to my referral request?

5. Should I learn answers to combat a "no" to my referral request?

6. How often should I connect with my clients in order to keep referrals coming?

7. How many referrals should I get?

8. How do I keep my "A" clients giving really valuable referrals?

9. Can I just call referrals if I don't have a client introduction?

10. What's your best advice for improving my referral success?

Answers to the Most Frequently Asked Questions About Referrals

1. **How important is a three-part referral script to my success?** Most advisors ask for referrals (if they ask at all) based on momentary inspiration. Their requests are usually void of a participatory discussion of value, a value benefit for the referral and a security promise not to contact the referral unless both the client and advisor agree to an introduction process. If you are going to achieve maximum success in obtaining referrals, it is imperative that you communicate all three parts. It's no different from a golf swing. Learn to do it right and you will play with the top professionals; otherwise, you will always be a duffer with a few lucky strokes.

2. **Has the industry made referral asking more complicated than necessary?** Yes. Referral-getting has been made to look very complex … and it's not! It doesn't require hours and hours of training. The truth is that there are only three simple components for making an effective referral request. The rest is a personal courage decision. Understanding the simplicity of the skill will create greater success!

3. **How can I take the "scary" out of referral asking?** You can't, but you don't need to awfulize it out of proportion. Asking for referrals is scary for everyone at first. It's no different from playing a competitive sport. No matter how prepared you are, you are facing an unknown outcome. That is what makes

it scary. But you need to decide whether high-level success is your goal or whether you're willing to settle for mediocrity. If your goal is high-level success, it's time to say, "So what!" to your fear and do it anyway. Eventually you will find that getting referrals becomes easy and fun, though it will always remain an emotional challenge. Great agents decide that's okay and ask anyway.

4. **What do I do if my client says "no" to my referral request?** About 20% of all clients will say "no" to a referral request. Who cares? That should be your attitude. Keep your ego intact, your friendship alive, thank them for their consideration and move on. They won't think less of you for asking.

5. **Should I learn answers to combat a "no" to my referral request?** No! Learn to ask for referrals the right way and if you meet with a "no," don't beat yourself up. No need to waste time on second attempts. A "no" is okay and you can graciously back out. Not asking is not okay.

6. **How often should I connect with my clients in order to keep referrals coming?** If you don't connect at least 15 times per year, your clients will consider that it is neither their obligation to purchase their next product from you nor give you continued referrals. Failing to keep your promise of staying connected will leave you too embarrassed to ask, feeling that you don't deserve additional referrals. Keeping connected — continuously — is critical for giving you confidence to ask and keeping your client happy to reciprocate.

7. **How many referrals should I get?** Requesting a specific number from a client makes it a lot easier to accomplish the task. If you ask for five, it's easy to laugh with clients while telling them what a great job they are doing and that you only have two left to go. I, personally, would ask for five, but you may decide to ask for three. Whatever you decide, ask for a specific number of referrals and then commit to getting a certain number each month (15 is a reasonable goal).

8. **How do I keep my "A" clients giving really valuable referrals?** You can't maintain client loyalty or a sense of obligation if you aren't extending yourself continually in ways that are surprising and delightful. "A" clients don't give ongoing referrals just because you did a good job last year. "A" clients give referrals to people who stay connected and do things that are unexpected, exceptionally thoughtful, out of the ordinary and personally beneficial. This requires that you think out a connection strategy each year for your best "A" clients. When you do that, you invoke the rule of reciprocation. They want to pay you back, and giving a referral is an easy way to do so — especially if they feel certain that their friend will be treated likewise.

9. **Can I just call referrals if I don't have a client introduction?** In doing so, you will have just wasted some very valuable effort. Calling referrals without a personal introduction will incur significantly poorer results. It takes no effort to ask a client for an email introduction. If you are

using e-Relationship™, just pick an introduction message that is ghost-written for the client, send it to your client for approval to send to the list of their referrals, and ask the client to press the send button. The message is immediately sent and you just increased your appointment results fourfold.

10. **What's your best advice for improving my referral success?** Get involved with a large group of targeted prospects who: (1) have a common cause, (2) assemble together at least once a month (weekly or biweekly is better) and (3) have an interest that you share — church, civic group, community group or occupational association. When you get referred to people within the group, you will have far greater success in getting appointments and eventually being considered "the professional" within that group. Statistics indicate that 79% of people buy service products from people they have relationships with. The commonality strength of your connection delivers a tremendous advantage in getting clients to refer you to other members and provides the greatest level of emotional safety for prospects to accept your appointment request. Pick a group and get actively involved. An empty chair renders no preference.

CHAPTER
ONE

The Referral Mandate – Get Them!

My manager barked at me, "Be bolder in asking for referrals. Refuse to take no for an answer. Get the results. I don't want to hear about the labor pains, just show me the babies! No whining, no excuses. Just get referrals and commit yourself to get the number you ask for — *five!*"

After only a month in the business, those were the words my manager repeated to every newbie who entered the life insurance business. His drill sergeant manner didn't leave much room for questions, but I sensed he was right. However, it was my thirteenth selling appointment for the month, I had sold five policies and I just wanted to get my sixth sale. That was my focus. Sell another policy.

Though my focus was on the sale, my manager was relentless about referrals. Why? Because he knew that failing to get referrals would hinder my future success.

He was right. I had met many of our older agents in the office who were horrible at getting referrals, and their careers were mediocre at best. You probably know the same agents or advisors in your office. All their outcomes are identical. Mediocre.

No matter how successful you are, failing to get referrals will stop you from attaining your maximum potential.

I wanted more. I wanted to be truly successful. I knew I had to learn to get referrals … or maybe I just had to quit being such a wimp and start asking — not just once in a while but all the time. Maybe my problem was courage. Bravery. Whatever it was, I determined that if others could do it, so could I.

Maybe you're sensing that I was a little angry. That's good. Nothing happens until you get mad. So let it happen. Get mad. It's time. Claim your success. Stop the wimp-out factor. It's time to change.

CHAPTER TWO

Find Your Turning Point

My new client, a minor league basketball player, stood up to leave. His 6'5" frame hovered over me. Commenting that he needed to be on time for his practice, he was in an obvious hurry.

"Terry," I said, "sit down. We're not quite done. Go ahead ... sit down. Please. This won't take long."

I was nervous, but I knew it was time to stop making excuses to myself. I had to ask for referrals! Waiting until the next time I saw Terry, to deliver his policy, was just another excuse. *Now* was the time to ask, right after the sale ... not at delivery. Now was the best time, and I was going to stop wimping out.

"Terry, tell me what you liked best about what we have accomplished during this process. What was the most valuable outcome that you derived from our work together over the last few weeks?" I paused and waited for his answer.

A value agreement is always the first element of an effective referral request.

Terry responded, "I really liked how we put a plan together that took care of some issues that I really wasn't giving enough attention to. I know my wife appreciates the additional insurance we purchased and even the small amount of money we are putting into the mutual fund will eventually make a difference."

He glanced nervously at his watch, but I forged on. "Terry, I really appreciate your becoming a new client, and my promise is to stay in touch and keep you up-to-date throughout the years as we continue to build on your program and keep your objectives attainable. But adding you as a client has actually created a major problem for me. Do you know what that is?"

He looked a little befuddled. "I thought your job is to sell insurance and investment products. I think you did that pretty well."

"It is, but when someone becomes a client, that means I have just lost a prospect. Becoming a client diminishes the number of prospects I have to call on … and that is a problem." I chuckled as I added, "One that you have now caused for me.

"Terry, if I have to concentrate too much on looking for prospects, I can't spend as much time as I would like keeping in touch with clients, like you. So I need you to help me out of this dilemma. I want you to think of some people who might be good clients for me someday. I am going to ask you to replace yourself as a prospect."

"But Bob," he insisted. "I'm going to be late for my practice."

With a determined push in my voice, mellowed with slight laughter, I replied, "Terry, if we do this fast, you won't be late for your practice. So help me out here. We can do this fast or slow. It's totally up to you. I need five names. Let's start with one name. Who's the first person that comes to mind? Who's your best friend? Your closest teammate? Let's start there.

"Great. Now ... if you and your best friend were going to invite two more friends to golf, or to attend the annual Final Four basketball tournament, who would you invite?"

Terry gave me two more names and then stood up, announcing that he had to leave. I told him that I understood, but could he think of two more names while I followed him to his car? Heading toward the door with me on his heels, he gave me another name. I thanked him and said, "Okay, that leaves just one more. Terry, it isn't going to help you if you become a client and I someday can't pay enough attention to you because I am looking for prospects. Give me one more name, that's all I need. We'll be done and you will be off to practice."

When asking for referrals, give your client a description of someone you would consider a quality prospect.

He gave me a quick last name while sliding into his car seat, we shook hands, and he headed to practice.

Seven weeks later Terry's policy arrived, and I called to set a time to deliver it. When we met, he asked how his referrals had worked out. He told me he had laughed and shaken his head at my tenacity as he drove away from our last meeting. And then, without being prompted, he offered me another name, number six, to add to his previous referrals. He had appreciated my determination!

Clients appreciate advisors who show a tenacity to be successful. Don't be timid.

That verbal exchange had produced what my manager demanded — but it made an even bigger impact on my psyche. I had internalized what all big producers know and what mediocre agents continue to wimp out at: that referrals are the life blood of superior production and, without them, you are limited.

Asking for referrals begins with courage — your willingness to face the unknown. There is no excuse that will suffice for not getting referrals. Without referrals, it is only a matter of time before you're just another mediocre producer in the financial services business.

I never chickened out again. Referrals were no longer a hopeful wish. This was the way I did business. It was my choice to change. Now it's your turn.

Why not make today your turning point?

CHAPTER THREE

The Dynamics of How to Ask for Referrals

Getting referrals requires more than sheer personality coupled with a moment of inspiration. There are three components that must be present to deliver an effective referral talk to your client. Altogether, they deliver a psychological comfort for clients who are considering whether to refer you to their friends. You can change the words to accommodate your style, but don't omit any of the three components — not if you want to maximize your referral results.

COMPONENT NO. 1:
Value Agreement

Get your client reinvested in the value of the work you have just completed. This is a collaborative process, a two-way shared conversation, if you want true buy-in as to the value of what has been accomplished. Your client may have just purchased your recommendation but unless you help him or her visualize the entirety of the overall process, the focus maintains only on what has occurred over the last 30 minutes.

Immediately after the sale, start the conversation by summarizing what you think the value was — and then ask for comments. Without this verbal expression from the client, you don't have a value agreement that has substance to carry the referral conversation forward.

COMPONENT NO. 2:

The "Stay in Touch" Guarantee (Clients and Referrals)

Guarantee your commitment to stay in touch with occasional phone calls and monthly financial tips, and then take that guarantee a step further by explaining that you treat referrals in the same way, as privileged clients. You are now offering to give, instead of get. It delivers a lot of goodwill, increases the emotional safety for a client to give names of friends, and sets you apart from the masses.

E-Relationship™ is the #1 email connection tool in the financial industry. The name of every referral should be placed in the database, where monthly financial tips and suggestions will drip on these potential clients throughout the year. This continuous connection is not only appreciated by your clients, but sets you apart from the all-too-typical financial advisor who only connects twice a year – the typical offer of an annual review and a birthday wish. You can see a demo at www.e-relationship.com.

If you want to expand your goodwill after completing an application for a new sale, give the client something that has personal value — and then offer to do the same for anyone they refer to you.

You might give them, for example, a copy of Family Love Letter, by John Scroggin and Donna Pagano (www.familyloveletter.com). This is a very classy repository book that helps individuals organize personal financial information, such as locations of safety deposit keys, important documents, lists of assets, insurance coverage, professionals who handle their financial affairs, family directives, and special provisions for loved ones. It also has a section for favorite family memories and photos. Family Love Letter is a beautiful gift that's as much a legacy of one's life as it is a financial repository. Priced at under $10, it's guaranteed to surprise and delight, as well as re-invoke the rule of reciprocation when you ask for referrals.

When you do something that is deemed to be remarkable (surprising), relevant and personal, you invoke the rule of reciprocation — a feeling of obligation by the other person to respond in kind. Many agents make the mistake of thinking that their financial work deserves to be rewarded (or reciprocated) with referrals. Clients, on the other hand, feel they have already reciprocated — they gave you a check for your recommendation! But when we extend ourselves with a surprise, one that has meaning and is special to the client, the whole process of reciprocation starts over.

COMPONENT NO. 3: Discussion of Friends

Ask permission to brainstorm with your client about friends they believe might benefit from your work ... while giving assurances that you will not contact them unless you both agree they would be a good fit for your practice and you also both agree on the introduction process. When you set this discussion up as a brainstorm, it takes all the pressure off you and the client. "We're just brainstorming here. I won't make contact unless you and I agree on how to get introduced."

Describe the type of prospect that best complements your work. Start the discussion by suggesting a category of people (e.g., business owner, a family with income over a certain level, an employer with at least 10 employees) or bring up the name of someone you believe they may know. When a name is given, ask information about the person, what's going on in their life, why this could be a good person for you to meet, and how an introduction might be initiated.

When discussing introductions, many clients will prefer to give you an email introduction. It is easy to orchestrate and requires little effort on anyone's behalf. Make sure you emphasize that even if the introductions do not immediately generate meetings, you will still treat these referrals as though they are privileged clients, offering to include them in your frequent or monthly emails regarding financial tips and information throughout the year.

Consider getting involved in at least one specific occupational (e.g., home builders, dentists), civic (Rotary), community (chamber of commerce), or religious target market. If a client is also in this organization, pull out the membership list, explain that you will eventually be calling on all of these people, and ask for three or four names of persons they personally know and believe might be great contacts. Focus your work in a specific group and your professional reputation can soar, along with your referrals.

Be professionally persistent when asking for referrals. Don't wimp out. Your clients will actually admire your determination. Believe that everyone can give you at least three names – and that will become the minimum you will normally get.

CHAPTER
FOUR

The Referral Script for Today's Client

Having a system for getting referrals is different from what it was just a few short years ago. Using newer processes will find your client receptive and cooperative, while older, traditional processes will cause inferior results. Though no process will produce results all the time, the right process will generate a 75–85% success rate. Why not 100%? Because no system will produce results in every single case. The complexity of human nature will prevent that.

Accept the fact that some people won't give you a referral regardless of how you ask and that others you thought would decline your request will be your biggest advocates. Your job is not to contemplate which client you are going to ask. Your job is to *ask* every client! Internalize in your mind that not asking is unacceptable. It is the unpardonable sin! Don't make it. Ask!

If you're not getting referrals, you're not asking. Courage is 80% of the formula.

So … what should you say? Without a script, you're dependent on momentary inspiration and that will cause hesitation and inferior results. Any single script is better than the best daily inspiration. A script is not for beginners. A script is for professionals. A well-designed script is just as valuable to your referral success as learning a golf stroke would be to your golf game. Though pro golfers all differ slightly in how they stroke the ball, they learn the basics and then practice to perfection their own personal style. It's the same stroke, hole after hole. Learn a professional script so that you have no hesitation in your effectiveness. It's your path to greatest success. Your anxiety in getting referrals will disappear and your results will soar.

A suggested three-part script:

COMPONENT NO. 1:
Value Agreement

"When we began working together, we started our process by talking about some of your big-picture goals, objectives, and concerns. Then we reflected on today's challenges and took a more specific look at what you had already implemented. I think that provided a great foundation for developing value recommendations to make your financial goals even more attainable.

Without the client adding personal comments as to the value of the process, you don't have a value agreement that has substance to carry the referral conversation forward.

"Without putting words in your mouth, where do you feel the greatest value of our work has been for you?" (Wait for an answer. The client must expand the conversation with his or her thoughts about the value of the process.)

"What did you like most about how the whole process was handled?"

COMPONENT NO. 2:
The "Stay in Touch" Guarantee (Clients and Referrals)

"One of the core principles of my business is my guarantee to stay in touch each month, through the sharing of important financial information and tips — and it's a guarantee I make not only to my clients but also to friends my clients refer to me.

Offering to give value to a referral, even if you don't get an appointment, increases a client's emotional safety, delivers a lot of goodwill, and places professional respect for you well above what the client considers to be the typical financial advisor in the market.

"I treat all referrals as though they were already privileged clients. I offer to send them the same monthly financial tips and messages that I send to my clients, especially if they think that's preferable before agreeing to meet. That gives them the opportunity to get to know me and the type of work I do before meeting face to face.

"Most of my clients really appreciate this low-key approach. If you were to refer someone to me, do you think your friends would appreciate that approach?"

COMPONENT NO. 3:
Discussion of Friends

"I do the majority of my business with two categories of people — first, people that I personally meet and, second, people my clients introduce me to. I want you to know that I never call anyone without first getting introduced to them in a way that we both feel they would appreciate. Most of my clients really appreciate that.

"With that being said, would you brainstorm with me on some friends or acquaintances you believe might benefit from my work? If we both think that they may be good contacts, you can then tell me if it would be best to get introduced in person, over the phone, or maybe through a simple email introduction. I will trust your judgment for that.

"Are there three, four, or five friends who come to mind (suggest a prospect category or a name to get them started) who might be people for you and me to discuss?"

If the client is hesitant, repeat the following: "I am sure that your friends would at least appreciate receiving my monthly financial information as a starter. They can then decide later if they would like to meet. Who's the first person that comes to mind?"

Put the names of all your clients and prospects into your e-Relationship™ database (www.e-relationship.com). This is also the perfect place to put referrals who say no to your appointment request. Never lose a prospect!

Automate the connection process. It will send seven e-storyboards on financial topics each year, four quarterly financial e-checklists, four holiday e-cards, four motivational e-newsletters, a birthday e-card and a wedding anniversary e-card.

This consistent connection builds emotional safety, appreciation and market separation as compared to the typical advisor. Outclass the expected and you will win the client.

CHAPTER FIVE

When Your Referral Request Is Denied

Twenty-five percent of newly sold clients will say no to a referral request. It's not because you didn't ask correctly or weren't persistent enough or didn't have a clever answer to their objection. There are a myriad of reasons people will say no, and most of them have to do with their own life influences. In other words, a no is about them; it's not about you. Don't beat yourself up or feel like a failure. Just accept that some people will say no and that's that!

Ask ... Ask ... Ask! Don't ever make an excuse. This is critical to your level of business success.

What I don't want you to allow yourself to do is *not* ask ... even if you *think* the client is going to be difficult. That is being a wimp, and many times you will guess wrong! Some of your best referral names will come from clients you "thought" would have said no. Ask everyone. It's time to make it a habit.

Here is your job in a nutshell:

Ask for referrals ... *every time*.

Get referrals 75% of the time or you are wimping out.

Thank those who refuse to give you a referral and forget about it. The client's refusal is not your skill set. It is their life-story baggage. Don't let it be your problem.

The Two Guarantees
That Will Get Referrals

When clients hesitate to give referrals, it's usually because they're concerned that their friends will feel pressured to meet and their relationship with them, as a result, may suffer. You can largely eliminate this anxiety with two promise guarantees:

1. Guarantee that you will not contact their friends unless you both agree on how to be introduced. An email introduction requires little effort and is very effective. (www.e-relationship.com)

2. Guarantee that you will treat their hesitant friends as though they are privileged clients. If any referrals turn down your appointment request, offer to place them into your database so you can send monthly financial information as a way to better acquaint them with you and your services. If they conclude that your services are beneficial, a meeting can be arranged later. This is usually a well received approach.

Assuring your clients that you are sincerely interested in "giving" value to their friends, rather than only trying to "get" appointments, will open the door to better referral discussions. It will also guarantee that you will never again lose a hesitant prospect, many of whom will later become clients. Never lose a prospect!

CHAPTER SIX

Introductions to Referrals are Critical – Agree on the Process!

Getting the majority of your referrals to agree to an appointment is no longer about simply telling them about you and your company or that a client of yours is a friend of theirs. Name recognition of a friend may be sufficient for a few (a dwindling few) to agree to an appointment, but it is not enough for most. It takes more to have them feel emotionally safe to accept your appointment request.

Getting a referral name is no longer adequate. You *must* be equally committed to getting an introduction!

Obtaining a personal introduction is nothing short of imperative in today's skeptical world. Without one, surveys show, fewer than 20% of your referral appointment requests will be successful. Even if your average is higher, it won't exceed the percentage of appointments you will get with a personal introduction — over 85%! Personal referral introductions give you four times more appointments throughout the year and account for significantly larger sales.

There are only four ways to get personally introduced.

Face-to-Face: If the referred person works in the same office as your client, a face-to-face introduction may be a simple request. Or you may offer to take them both to lunch where a personal introduction can be made.

By Phone: When you're with a client, you may ask him or her to call a friend and introduce you. After a brief introduction, the client hands the phone to you and you can request an appointment or suggest a lunch meeting.

Letter from the Client: Have the client agree to a letter of introduction that you have typed on his or her stationary for the people referred. This will require setting up another meeting to have the client sign the letters before mailing. (Don't cut this method short by sending a pre-approach letter from you with the client's name mentioned. This is very ineffective.)

By Email: Using an email from your client to a referral can provide the easiest and most effective introduction. It requires little effort by you or your client — and if you know when the referred person receives the email (unlike postal mail), placing a call within the hour can result in appointments about 80% of the time.

After brainstorming with the client about friends who might benefit from your work, it is simple to say, "As I mentioned before, I only call on people you refer to me when we decide together how to get introduced. In other words, I would like to discuss ways that you think would work for an introduction.

It's critical that you ask the client to give you an introduction as part of your referral procedure. Without an introduction, over 80% of referral contacts decline appointment requests.

"I am fine if we want to arrange lunch with one or two of your friends. Or I would be glad to put together a quick email introduction message that I could send to you. If you like it, you only have to click the send button and it will send the email to your friend and a message to me to let me know that it was received. I can then call and suggest that I would be glad to meet them or to simply include them in my future mailings. Whatever works for them is fine for me.

"What introduction method do you think would be easiest for you and work best?"

E-Relationship™ is the #1 utilized email referral module in the financial industry. The agent simply chooses from a number of pre-written intro-duction messages and sends it to the client for approval. The client then only has to click the send button to mail it to a friend, and you are notified when the email is received. The phone call to the referral is easy, effective and fun. You will receive compliments from both the referral and the client. See a demo at www.e-relationship.com.

CHAPTER SEVEN

Creating Clients to Become Consistent Referral Givers

It is unfortunate that most agents have relatively few clients (or none) who become dependable sources for ongoing referrals during their careers. Even those clients who gave referrals seem to fade away and, over time, agents justifiably believe they will come up empty-handed if they ask them for more. The solution is not about reminding the client about the quality work you do, but rather establishing an ongoing sense of personal gratitude.

Many agents make the mistake of believing that they only need to do a good job, send a birthday card once a year, and follow up with an annual review phone call — and in return the client will be happy to continually reward them with more referrals. That is not the case. Nothing in that combination of contact is unique. It is no more than we expect from our dentist, chiropractor, or pet veterinarian and it doesn't create a sense of obligation.

Creating an ongoing flow of referrals from a select group of clients requires that you continue to invoke the rule of reciprocation. Definition: We repay in kind what other people do for us that is considered of personal benefit. To further that definition, "personal benefit" means that they consider the act of kindness to be intended just for them, or for a select group of people you have extended yourself to in a special way that has nothing to do with business.

Society teaches an implied agreement of reciprocity when an act of personal kindness is extended. For example, when invited to a dinner party, we take a bottle of wine or flowers. Even if the host and hostess tell us not to bring a thing, we don't go empty-handed. Many of us even have gift closets in order to repay quickly an unexpected act of kindness.

The lesson is: If you want your top 10 or 20 clients to become ongoing referral sources, you must extend yourself to them at least three times a year in ways that are personally unique, relevant and surprising.

Examples of Surprising Events

• Have an annual appreciation dinner at your home for your top 10 clients. Don't ruin the sense of reciprocation by giving a 20-minute talk on the economy, or having a guest speaker, or passing out information on your newest planning technique or investment idea. That turns the event into a business event, not an appreciation event. It is now for your benefit, not theirs. It will incur no sense of reciprocity. If you want to do an annual economic update at the country club with cocktails once a year, that's fine, but it will not be considered a personal act of kindness that incurs a sense of obligation to pay you back. They paid you back by attending!

- Hold an annual summer home barbeque for your top 10 clients. Keep all business out of the affair.

- Deliver trays of homemade cookies or baked goods to your client's home (or office) on a set day that you announce as your annual Top 10 Client Appreciation Week or Day.

- Deliver an annual personalized birthday cake to your top 10 clients at their office — not just a card. Do it every year and you will find that this is a home run.

- Deliver a pumpkin cheese cake to your top 10 clients the Monday or Tuesday before Thanksgiving.

- Invite your best clients to your home for an annual potluck dessert event during the Holidays or to a Kentucky Derby Party every May.

- Deliver canisters of popcorn two days before New Year's Day. The surprise factor for this holiday creates tremendous appreciation and market separation — your benefit!

- For less than $100, purchase 10 copies of Family Love Letter, written by John Scroggin, AEP, JD, LL.M., and Donna Pagano, CFP. (www.familyloveletter.com) Deliver these books either around Thanksgiving or the holidays and then schedule a lunch with the client during the next week. At lunch, ask for referrals and promise to give their friends a copy.

My Favorite – and Most Effective – Idea

This idea requires little effort on your part, incurs very little cost, and is highly effective — plus you don't need to worry about your favorite clients not attending due to a conflict in their schedules. I suggest that you implement this idea for your top 20 clients and build the client circle for at least one year to include every new sale that generates a minimum amount of commissions, such as $1,000. The outlay is less than the cost of lunch once a year, will impact your client 12 times per year, and will keep you top of mind in a very personal way. Many agents have more than 100 clients on this idea, and every year we hear about how successful it has been for attracting ongoing referrals from appreciative clients.

Purchase subscriptions to either Budget Travel or Islands Magazine for your Top 20 clients and any new client whose sale generated at least $1,000 in commissions. A gift subscription is only $12 per year. (If purchased off the shelf, the magazines would cost $60 to $90.) Every two years change the magazine — no idea generates gratitude forever and a change in magazine always incurs another thank-you and keeps the rule of reciprocity at high levels.

Put the recipient's name on the gift subscription form and put "Gift from (your name)" on the first address line. Put the client's address on the second address line to complete the form.

If you don't use this idea for your top 10 or 20 clients … then I am not sure why you have read this book! Do this by tomorrow or you have just missed the best idea in the industry for keeping clients loyal and providing ongoing referrals!

In other words, if your name is Sam Jones, the mailing label on the magazine received by your client will read: client name, "Gift from Sam Jones," client address. This means that 12 times a year your clients will see a label on their magazines and be reminded that you were responsible for this act of kindness. Don't send the magazine to their places of business — send it to their homes!

The magazine must be a travel magazine. Travel magazines have the longest shelf life (17 months) and are regarded as having nothing to do with your business. It is truly a personal act of kindness. If you change the magazine to anything business, it negates the personal benefit and is regarded as a benefit to you, not them.

The appreciation, continual visibility, and deep loyalty that this simple little idea builds will result in numerous additional sales and referrals. For $10 to $15 per year, this idea is a home run.

Test this idea with 10 of your best clients. Call them a few times a year for referrals and watch how they try to help you. You are keeping in touch as a friend — it's not just about business. Your contact is consistent and the appreciation impact is huge. It just doesn't get any easier than this.

Examples of the Magazine Letter
to Your Client

Dear [Existing Top 20 Client],

You are an especially valued client and I want to thank you for your business and the confidence you have placed in me. To express my appreciation and to let you know how much I value you as one of my top clients, I have ordered a subscription for you to Budget Travel Magazine. I hope you enjoy it.

In the event you are wondering, there is no catch in receiving this magazine. It is just one way for me to recognize my favorite clients. I am grateful for your business, but even more so ... our friendship.

Let's stay in touch and over the course of the next year, don't keep me a secret. A great referral is always appreciated.

Sincerely,

Dear [New Client after the Sale],

I welcome you as a new client and again want to thank you for your business, the confidence you have placed in me, and the referrals to a few of your friends. To express my appreciation, I have ordered a subscription for you to Budget Travel Magazine. I hope you enjoy it.

In the event you are wondering, there is no catch in receiving this magazine. It is just one way for me to recognize my favorite clients in a special way. I am grateful for your business, but even more so … our new friendship that I hope continues to grow.

Let's stay in touch and over the course of the next year, don't keep me a secret. Feel free to brag about me to your friends. And remember, a great referral is always appreciated.

Sincerely,

60-Day Follow-Up Phone Call

Hello _____. I just wanted to give you a quick call and make sure you received your first issue of the Budget Travel Magazine I ordered for you. Have you gotten it yet? Great! Hey ... what's your schedule like this week? Why don't we grab lunch?

MAGAZINE ORDER FORM:

Dear Sir/Madam,

Below is a list of Budget Travel Magazine subscriptions we are giving as gifts to our top clients and prospects this year. We would like the subscriptions to begin [MONTH/YEAR]. Please print the address labels *exactly* as shown *below. Please bill these new subscriptions to:*

Your Name
Your Address
City, State Zip

Send form to:
BUDGET TRAVEL®
PO Box 5603
Harlan, IA 51593-3103

OR CALL:
1-800-829-9161

Sincerely,

[Your Name]

[Your Telephone Number]

MAGAZINE GIFT RECIPIENTS:

Full Name: [Recipient Name]

Address 1: *Gift from* [Your Name]

Address 2: [Recipient Street Address]

City, State Zip:

Full Name: [Recipient Name]

Address 1: *Gift from* [Your Name]

Address 2: [Recipient Street Address]

City, State Zip:

Full Name: [Recipient Name]

Address 1: *Gift from* [Your Name]

Address 2: [Recipient Street Address]

City, State Zip:

E-Relationship™ keeps in touch with all your clients at least 10 to 15 times a year!

Experience proves that you can't build significant client loyalty and stimulate ongoing referrals by only placing an occasional phone call to a client, offering to conduct an annual review, or sending an occasional business newsletter. Client contact needs to be more frequent and remarkably more distinctive than what the client would expect from the typical financial advisor relationship.

Building a committed relationship requires using separate strategies to both accentuate your business focus and keep you personally connected each and every year. Without using electronic communication for contact (www.e-relationship.com), you won't stay connected frequently enough to maintain loyalty. Neither will you feel entitled to ask established clients for referrals in the future.

When you lose frequent contact, you know you don't deserve referrals. Go to www.e-relationship.com and view the demo that shows how to automate 15 connections per year. It's inexpensive and it will make a big impact on referrals, as well as uncover numerous sales that often go undetected.

PROLOGUE

It is now up to you.

There is no elongated course on referral-getting that is going to provide the "little secret" we left out of this book.

There is no script that is going to provide better words.

There is no coaching that will provide an epiphany of wisdom.

There is no weekly accountability group that will make up for your lack of bravery.

There is no more.

Referral success is a personal decision.

It's a turning point.

It is all about courage.

It is all about *you* — your determination and commitment.

Will you do it?

Only you can answer that question.

Remember … It's just NOT that hard!

Customize Your Referral Request and Your Top Client Connection Strategy

Write a script to use in requesting referrals. Create a paragraph for each of the three components.

COMPONENT NO. 1:
Value Agreement

Review the process and ask for their expression of value. *When we began working together, we started out by ...*

_____

_____

_____

_____

_____

_____

_____

_____

_____

_____

_____

_____

COMPONENT NO. 2:

The "Stay in Touch" Guarantee
(Clients and Referrals)

One of the core principles of my business is …

_____

_____

_____

_____

_____

_____

COMPONENT NO. 3:

Discussion of Friends

Who is someone that comes to mind that (describe ideal candidate) …

_____

_____

_____

_____

_____

_____

_____

Your Introduction Script

AGREEMENT ON HOW TO GET INTRODUCED

First of all, I want you to know that I never call someone who's been referred to me without ...

Surprising Events

Make a list of ongoing personal surprise events that you will commit to conducting with your top 10 or 20 clients. If you want continual referrals, your clients need to feel continually appreciated in special ways.

ADVISOR TOOLBOX

Competitive products are no longer unique. Advanced support is not a differentiator. Hope is not a strategy.

Take a day to build an attraction strategy, be consistent in implementation, and watch your reputation soar above the norm.

It is the wise business person who dares to open his or her mind to new ways of capturing clients and outperforming the competition.

Allow me to introduce you to a powerful set of programs and tools created by Identity Branding that will give you the inspiration, motivation and skills to be consistently successful.

Please...Make ME a little bit FAMOUS!
A Must Read!

In this book, Robert offers a cutting-edge approach to creating prospect attraction in today's skeptical marketplace. His first book, Identity Branding—Creating Prospect Attraction, was reprinted four times and is still used in study groups all over America. This new book takes the practical advice even further. It has over 180 pages describing in detail the newest prospect attraction strategies – examples that show sales professionals how to open doors to desirable prospects and make themselves a little bit FAMOUS in their local communities.

Please...Make ME a little Bit FAMOUS!
Complete Marketing Kit

Robert Krumroy's acclaimed financial industry book Please...Make ME a little bit FAMOUS is now available on CD, with 21 mini-marketing booklets as a bonus. This marketing kit is a must-have if you want to build dominant recognition in your local community. Each of the booklets reveals an awareness strategy used by super achievers to build recognition, surprise, delight and appreciation with prospects and clients. Just choose or adapt the strategy that fits your personality and market. All of the information you need to implement a strategy (including sample letters and order forms) are included here. It's an unbeatable way to learn how to open doors in your market.

The Prospect Relationship Ladder

Old traditional methods of "getting in" don't work — not like they use to; even better phone approaches produce minimal improvements. Today's methods and systems for gaining prospect access are new and must be learned. Helping your prospect climb the Relationship Ladder to the Emotional Safety Rung will cause your appointment success to soar ... as well as significantly impact your sales! Read this book.

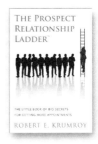

It's NOT About Luck!

Impression management is the new skill for creating prospect attraction and solving your advisor's appointment activity challenge. As a manager, nothing will cause greater appointment and production increases than directing your advisors in building effective prospect-attraction strategies. When done correctly, clients will increase their loyalty and prospects will enthusiastically agree to appointments with your advisors,

concluding that they are remarkable and far superior to the competition. Apply this new skill and watch your advisor's activity, production, retention, recruiting and your firm's reputation soar to new heights.

Identity Branding Revisited—Creating Prospect Attraction
For Financial Planners and Insurance Agents

Already in its fourth printing, this is the most talked about marketing book in the financial industry. Within 9 months of being released, a second printing was required. Over 200 pages that give you the secrets to creating a visible differentiation in the marketplace; a client perception of superior value; a consumer preference for you.

Don't miss this powerful book.

Brilliant Strategies and Fatal Blunders
This book is a must read!

Working hard, providing a quality product or being personally determined to "gut it out" until people recognize your expertise and give you their business no longer attains high-level success. High-level success requires critical thinking; building visible market differentiation; and then outclassing the competition. This book identifies the brilliant strategies used by professionals, service companies and retail establishments to do just that ... beat the competition and thrive. But caution, the fatal blunders are practically invisible and almost always terminal. If you want to survive and thrive, read this book.

Sell the Problem
This book is a must read!

Have you missed a sale lately? Did you do a poor job presenting your solution ... or the problem? Most advisors don't sell the problem adequately before attempting to sell their solution. The prospect must buy the cost of the problem first! Learn to sell the pain, the loss and the unwanted consequences of the problem and you will have an easy time selling the solution.

Marketing Booklets

Every advisor has a "getting in" problem in today's environment. Prospects, even referrals, are hesitant to say "yes" to an appointment request. The bottom line is if you want to solve the "getting in" problem, you must apply a "getting in" solution. Separating you from the competition requires differentiation and high-level consistent visibility. Consistent visibility is the hallmark of attraction. Heightening awareness of you and your differentiated business reputation is critical for gaining attraction. Frequent visibility is imperative if you expect the majority of your appointment requests to be accepted. Robert Krumroy, President of Identity Branding/e-Relationship™, has developed Creating Prospect Approachability Booklets, which provide ideas that produce exceptional results.

Please…Make ME a little bit FAMOUS!
The Prospect Attraction Workshop

- *Increase Sales!*
- *Obtain Welcomed Appointments!*
- *Raise Your Referral Rate!*
- *Develop a 1-Year Personal Branding Plan!*
- *Attain Greater Career Satisfaction!*

In this concise and lively program, we teach you how to create a market attraction strategy that elevates your personal visibility, professional image, confidence and prospect approachability. The workshop is available in either a 2½-hour or five-hour format and includes a 14-page workbook for each participant. The agenda includes:

1 History

What has changed in the marketplace? It isn't an illusion; it is harder to get in to see prospects than any time in history … and old techniques aren't working. The advisor must learn and engage the six new psychological rules of attraction to achieve high-level success.

2 Engage Your Targeted Prospects

Teaching advisors how to heighten their local market attraction and credibility through uniquely engaging their prospect clusters will build likeability and market separation. These strategies increase advisors' confidence, as well as prospect approachability.

The session ends with each advisor identifying a strategic event(s) that he or she will embrace to build personal local recognition and affection to a specific audience.

3 Character Uniqueness

Identify ways that advisors can tightly bond to their top 20 clients and centers of influence. The result is increased sales and a continuous flow of invaluable referrals throughout the year. Once a strategy is implemented, advisors will improve their positioning, image, differentiation, referral flow and visibility to their top clients and targeted prospects.

4 Staying Connected

Out of sight, out of mind! Getting and staying connected to prospects and clients is the foundation of attraction and creating deep client loyalty. There is no more effective way to open doors, build market separation and establish superior credibility than by delivering consistent "top of mind" touch points. If you want increased appointments and welcomed access to new prospects, learn the secrets to effective connection.

The number-one e-connection tool in the financial industry!

Consistent connection is one of the mainstays of being a highly successful financial advisor. Our e-Relationship™ automated email program makes it delightfully easy to keep in touch with every prospect and client in your database. Send holiday e-cards, e-birthday wishes, e-newsletters and more throughout the year. Also choose from 75 prepackaged financial e-briefs. Each message is personalized and sent one at a time—no multiple-name mailing list is ever seen by your recipients.

www.e-relationship.com

PLEASE PROVIDE INFORMATION ON:

❏ Prospect Attraction Workshops ❏ Speaking Engagements

BOOKS:

❏ *Referrals Made Easy*... $7^{95} _____
❏ *Sell the Problem — The Prospect Will Beg For A Solution!*..... $9^{95} _____
❏ *The Prospect Relationship Ladder*................................. $16^{95} _____
❏ *Please...Make ME a little bit FAMOUS!*....................... $24^{95} _____
❏ *Please...Make ME a little bit FAMOUS! Audio Version*..... $39^{95} _____
❏ *Identity Branding – Revisited*..................................... $19^{95} _____
❏ *Brilliant Strategies and Fatal Blunders*.......................... $18^{95} _____
❏ *It's NOT About Luck!* (Manager Book).......................... $39^{95} _____

MARKETING KIT:

❏ *Please...Make ME a little bit FAMOUS!*
Complete Marketing Kit (Includes 21 Idea Booklets).............. $99^{95} _____

PAYMENT INFORMATION

Name _____ Phone Number _____

Company _____

Email Address _____

Office Mailing Address _____

City _____ State _____ Zip Code _____

Card Number _____ Expiration Date _____

Signature _____

❏ AMEX ❏ MasterCard ❏ VISA ❏ Discover ❏ Invoice Me

NOTE: Additional S/H charges will apply.

Fax to 336-303-7318
Identity Branding, Inc.
3300 Battleground Avenue, Suite 250, Greensboro, NC 27410
www.identitybranding.com / www.e-relationship.com
800-851-8169